Harvest Time

Ted Schaefer

Rourke
Publishing LLC
Vero Beach, Florida 32964

www.rourkepublishing.com

PHOTO CREDITS: © Magnus Lindh: title page; © Bruce Livingston: pages 5, 21 (tomato); © Alex Blako: pages 7, 21 (cabbage); © Jean Scheijen: pages 9, 21 (pepper); © Matt Williams: pages 9, 21 (corn); © Jamie Wilson: page 5; © Danny Chan: pages 10, 21 (potato); © Harris Shiffman: pages 11, 21 (onion); © Jostein Hauge: pages 11, 21 (carrot); © Murat Baysan: pages 13, 21 (bean); © Anita Patterson: page 18; © Jim Jurica: page 19; © Michael Connors: page 22

Editor: Robert Stengard-Olliges

Cover design by Nicola Stratford.

Library of Congress Cataloging-in-Publication Data

Schaefer, Ted, 1948-
  Harvest time / Ted Schaefer.
     p. cm. -- (My first math)
  Includes index.
  ISBN 1-59515-975-4 (harcover)
  ISBN 1-59515-946-0 (paperback)
  1. Counting--Juvenile literature. 2. Harvesting--Graphic methods--Juvenile literature. I. Title.
  QA113.S3828 2007
  513.2'11--dc22
                                        2006019779

Printed in the USA

CG/CG

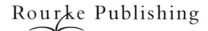

Rourke Publishing

www.rourkepublishing.com – sales@rourkepublishing.com
Post Office Box 3328, Vero Beach, FL 32964

Table of Contents

Pick the Vegetables   4

Pie Graph   15

Bar Graph   17

Picture Graph   21

Glossary   23

Index   24

Pick the Vegetables

It's **harvest** time! Time to pick the **vegetables** from our garden.

Today, I picked five red tomatoes and one green cabbage.

My sister picked seven red peppers and twelve ears of yellow corn.

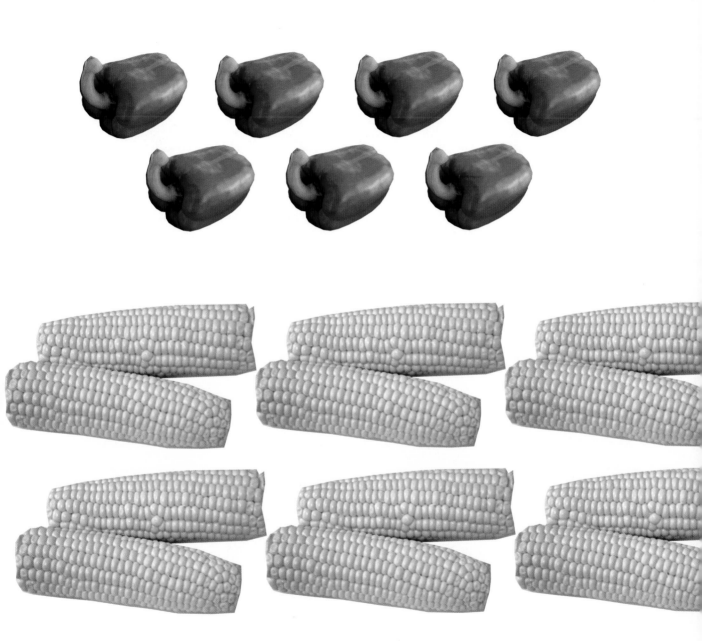

My dad dug twenty white potatoes, five white onions, and five orange carrots.

My mom picked forty-five green beans.

Altogether we harvested one hundred vegetables.
Who picked the most vegetables?

Me

5	Tomatoes
+ 1	Cabbage
6	

My Sister

7	Peppers
+12	Ears of Corn
19	

Dad

20	Potatoes
5	Onions
+ 5	Carrots
30	

Mom

45	Green Beans

Pie Graph

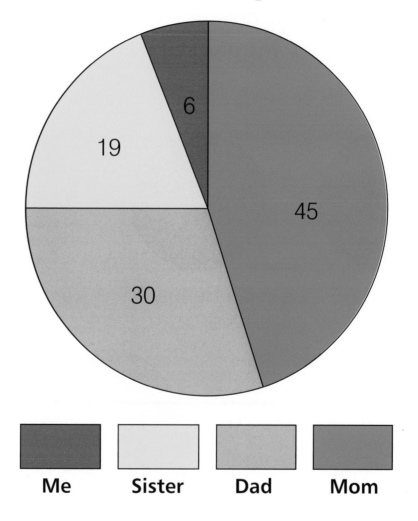

| Me | Sister | Dad | Mom |

Answer: Mom picked the most vegetables.

We harvested many colors of vegetables. Which vegetable color did we harvest the most?

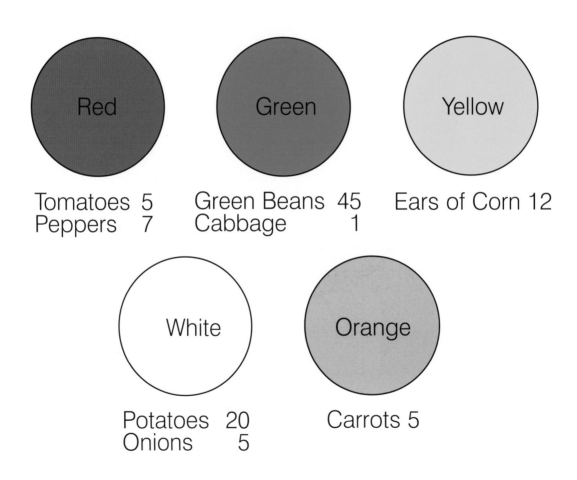

Red

Tomatoes 5
Peppers 7

Green

Green Beans 45
Cabbage 1

Yellow

Ears of Corn 12

White

Potatoes 20
Onions 5

Orange

Carrots 5

Bar Graph

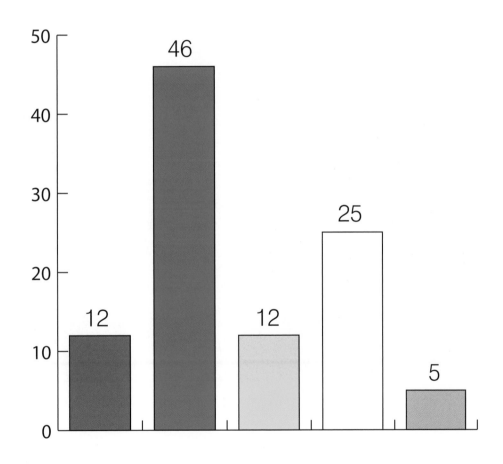

Answer: We harvested more green vegetables.

We picked vegetables above **ground** . . .

and dug vegetables from under the ground.

Did we harvest more vegetables from above or under the ground?

Picture Graph (or Pictograph)

Above Ground

Under Ground

We harvested more vegetables above ground.

Where are all the vegetables now? We made soup with some of the vegetables.YUMMMM!

Glossary

ground (GROUND) — dirt

harvest (HAR vist) — pick or gather crops

vegetables (VEJ tuh buhl) — any part of a plant that people eat that
  is not a fruit, nut, herb, spice, or grain

Index

garden   4
ground   18, 19, 20, 21
harvest   4, 14, 16, 17, 20
vegetable   4, 14, 15, 16, 17,18, 19, 20, 21, 22

Further Reading

Amato, William. *Math in the Kitchen.* Children's Press, 2002.
Beers, Bonnie. *Everyone Uses Math.* Yellow Umbrella Books, 2002.
Long, Lynette. *Great Graphs and Sensational Statistics.* John Wiley, 2004.

Websites To Visit

www.usda.gov/nass/nasskids/nasskids.htm
www.kidsgardening.com/2006.kids.garden.news/feb/pg1.html
www.pbs.org/teachersource/prek2/theme/graphing.shtm

About The Author

Ted Schaefer is both a writer and a woodworker. When he isn't researching and writing informational books for children, he is building furniture in his shop.